CHINESE ASTROLOGY

ASIAPAC COMIC SERIES

CHINESE ASTROLOGY

十 二 生 肖

BY SHERMAN TAI

■ Illustrated by Leow Yong Shin ■ Translated by Clara Show

ASIAPAC • SINGAPORE

Publisher
ASIAPAC BOOKS PTE LTD
629 Aljunied Road #04-06
Cititech Industrial Building
Singapore 389838
Tel: (65) 7453868
Fax: (65) 7453822
Email apacbks@singnet.com.sg

Visit us at our Internet home page
http://www.span.com.au/Asiapac.htm

First published February 1996
Reprinted April 1996

©1996 ASIAPAC BOOKS, SINGAPORE
ISBN 981-3029-93-5

Cover design by Cheng Yew Chung
Body text in 8/9 pt Helvetica
Printed in Singapore by
Chung Printing

Publisher's Note

Asiapac Books is proud to bring you this new comics on *Chinese Astrology - a general guide to the next 12 years of the animal cycle.* This easy-to-understand guide by Sherman Tai will help you to know more about yourself and the people close to you. The presentation is made more interesting by the comic illustrations provided by our young Malaysian artist Leow Yong Shin.

In the prologue, you will find out about the cycle of the 12 animals in Chinese astrology. You will learn how to identify your 'fortunate stem' and 'harmonious branch' as well as your own element. You will be interested to find out the personality, career prospects and interpersonal relationships of an individual born under each animal-sign. You will also be advised as to what to expect and also what to refrain from doing in each of the animal years. In the epilogue, you will see the link between fate and the 12 animals in Chinese astrology.

We would like to express our gratitude to Mr Sherman Tai for the opportunity to publish this valuable work; to Ms Clara Show for her translation; and the production team for putting in their best effort in the publication of this book.

About the Author

Sherman Tai is a graduate of the Hong Kong Technological University and furthered his studies in California, USA. He later embarked on a career in mechanical engineering and served in the He Ji-Huang Pu Group of Companies.

In his teens, Tai studied the Chinese art of divination under an expert. For more than 20 years, he researched extensively on the subject of Chinese astrology and *feng shui,* giving it a scientific and mathematical approach. In 1990, Tai emigrated to Canada and turned professional geomancer. His services are well sought-after by fellow emigrants who are anxious to know their destiny.

About The Illustrator

Leow Yong Shin, born in 1970, is a Malaysian artist of friendly disposition. After completing his secondary education in Malaysia, he began his career in Singapore working as an illustrator as well as a layout artist for one year and then as a draughtsman for more than two years.

Due to his keen interest in drawing comic characters, he has decided to pursue his career in the field of arts. Endowed with artistic talent coupled with a keen sense of perception and humour, he completed this volume, his first comic book, after one and a half years of self-study.

Introduction

A much-talked about subject in the Chinese community is the 12-animal cycle. Each person is born under a particular sign - the Rat, Tiger, Dragon, Horse, Pig, etc. And it is this sign that determines one's destiny. How one behaves and fares in his career, financial matters, marriage and health are directly linked to it.

In this book, the 12 animals are introduced in order of their appearance in the 12-year cycle and the unique characteristics of each, highlighted. For example, the Rat is intelligent, quick-thinking and highly adaptable whilst the Pig, being self-confident and self-centred, possesses leadership qualities. The book starts off with how each animal will fare in the Rat year (the first in the 12-year cycle) and moves on to the next 11, ending with the Pig year, giving a total of 144 subsections. The words are accompanied by comic illustrations to make this guide more reader-friendly and enjoyable.

Call it superstitious if you wish, but the Chinese have always been fascinated by this ancient art of divination and how accurate the predictions can be. Countless in-depth studies have been made on this subject and it will continue to intrigue many for years to come.

CONTENTS

Prologue: The 12 animals in Chinese astrology
To identify your 'fortunate stem' and 'harmonious branch'
To find your element

Epilogue: The link between the animals and one's fate
To believe or not to believe

Please identify your 'fortunate stem' and 'harmonious branch'.

Fortunate Stems

YIN 2 4 6 8 10

YANG 1 3 5 7 9

Harmonious Branches

1 Rat	5 Dragon	9 Monkey
2 Ox	6 Snake	10 Rooster
3 Tiger	7 Horse	11 Dog
4 Rabbit	8 Goat	12 Pig

TO FIND YOUR ELEMENT

The Five Elements	Fortunate Stems	Animal-Type
Metal	7, 8	Monkey, Rooster
Wood	1, 2	Tiger, Rabbit
Water	9, 10	Rat, Pig
Fire	3, 4	Snake, Horse
Earth	5, 6	Ox, Dragon, Goat, Dog

I'll give you 5 seconds to find your 'element'.

SPRING	1st lunar month	Tiger
	2nd lunar month	Rabbit
	3rd lunar month	Dragon
SUMMER	4th lunar month	Snake
	5th lunar month	Horse
	6th lunar month	Goat
AUTUMN	7th lunar month	Monkey
	8th lunar month	Rooster
	9th lunar month	Dog
WINTER	10th lunar month	Pig
	11th lunar month	Rat
	12th lunar month	Ox

RAT

Since olden times, the Rat has always been looked upon with disdain by man. Strangely enough, legend has it that the rodent originated from a falling star that fell onto earth centuries ago. It split into fragments which turned into numerous rats. Since then, the creature has had a profound effect on human beings.

THE RAT YEAR

Lunar Calendar	Element	Solar Calendar
1900	Earth	31 Jan 1900 - 18 Feb 1901
1912	Wood	18 Feb 1912 - 05 Feb 1913
1924	Metal	05 Feb 1924 - 23 Jan 1925
1936	Water	24 Jan 1936 - 10 Feb 1937
1948	Fire	10 Feb 1948 - 28 Jan 1949
1960	Earth	28 Feb 1960 - 14 Feb 1961
1972	Wood	15 Feb 1972 - 02 Feb 1973
1984	Metal	02 Feb 1984 - 19 Feb 1985
1996	Water	19 Feb 1996 - 06 Feb 1997

The Rat get along easily with those born in the year of the Monkey and Dragon.

The Ox and Dragon, especially the older ones and those of the opposite sex are the Rat's benefactor.

Where romance is concerned, the Rat should be wary of conflicts with those born in the year of the Horse.

CAREER

The Rat should not trust a fellow Rat and those born in the year of the Rabbit and Goat too much.

Trust us!

Crooks

People born in the Rat year tend to enter the service industry. Popular jobs for the males are in the field of advertising, music, mass media, research, tourism, food & beverage etc...

while the females consider careers in the beauty, fashion, film, hotel, food & beverage industries and writing to be ideal.

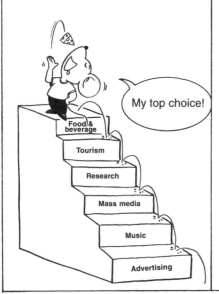

My top choice!

Food & beverage

Tourism

Research

Mass media

Music

Advertising

Food & beverage

Writing

Film

Fashion

Hotel

Beauty

Though the male and female are usually gentle and loving, they do not make good marriage partners. They have the tendency to be unfaithful.

The female's ideal partner should preferably be someone older and born in the year of the Dragon or Ox. The male's ideal partner should preferably be someone younger and born in the year of the Monkey or Dragon.

RAT IN THE RAT YEAR

The Rat Year heralds good fortune for the Rat. It is a year for making plans.

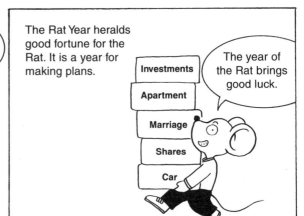

The year of the Rat brings good luck.

However, the Rat should not be too ambitious so as to avoid ending with nothing.

There goes my everything!

The Rat may suffer from allergies and respiratory problems in winter. Try to avoid visiting the sick or attending funeral ceremonies for it will erode your good fortune in the Rat year.

7

TIGER IN THE RAT YEAR

The Tiger will experience good fortune in the Rat year. This is especially true for males born in 1950 and 1974, and for females born in 1962.

Born: 1974

Born: 1950

Born: 1962

Very good!

Excellent progress can be expected where career and finance are concerned, particularly in spring.

promotion!

Despite the general good fortune, the Tiger should take plenty of rest. Health problems tend to occur in April and July. Be wary of accidents and try to avoid travelling overseas.

BANG!

I'm holding you responsible!

For the married, there is a tendency to get involved in extramarital affairs.

You asked for it, so don't blame me!

I'm doomed!

8

SNAKE IN THE RAT YEAR

There are signs of hidden danger and sorrow for the Snake in the Rat year.

February, March

Good!

May, June

July, October

Bad!

The favourable months are in February, March, May and June. However, July and October will bring about a broken relationship.

The self-employed and salaried workers will find that they gain very little in comparison to the efforts they put in. Money will come easily and go as easily. Students can expect good academic results.

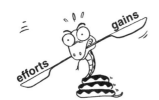

gains

efforts

But those hoping to find a life partner will be disappointed.

....

Proposal for marriage

HORSE IN THE RAT YEAR

It is a generally bad year for the Horse, especially in the autumn season. Those born in 1954 and 1966 have to be particularly careful about what they say or do.

Oh-o!...

Do not be stubborn or trust anyone readily. More often than not, your closest friends may turn out to be your worst enemies.

You take a sip first.

Oh no, I've added poison to it!

Health-wise, the Horse will constantly be under stress and suffer from insomnia. The problem can be alleviated by placing your bed with the headrest facing south.

Why did you place the bed in such an awkward position?

south

It will be a turbulent period for romance. Be wary of intrusion from a third party.

Leave him or let him be killed - it's all up to you!

third party

GOAT IN THE RAT YEAR

The Rat year holds very different fortunes for males and females born in the year of the Goat. The female will have exceptionally good fortune and be able to overcome all sorts of obstacles coming their way. This is especially true for those born in 1955 and 1967.

A good year for both of you!

As for the male, it will be a problematic year. Despite the hard work put in where career is concerned, there will not be any significant gains. Those born in 1943 and 1967 are the most affected ones.

You're in deep trouble!

Where romance is concerned, it will be a year of heartbreaks for the Goat.

I'm sorry to tell you I'm already married.

You cheated me of my feelings!

The Goat can be on the offensive in the months of Spring and Autumn but must prevent misfortune and sickness in the months of Winter. November and December are the times to watch out for signs of the flu and injuries to the limbs.

Meow!

Thanks for saving my life!

Oh, my arm hurts!

MONKEY IN THE RAT YEAR

It will be a plain sailing year for the Monkey with good prospects in career and finance. This is especially true for those born in 1956 and 1968.

Good!

Autumn and winter are the most favourable seasons, but there will be some obstacles in January and February.

Get out of my way!

January   February

Avoid stress brought on by overworking. Watch out for food-related illnesses in May and June.

How disgusting! Luckily, I have taken preventive measures.

Why are you in such a hurry to get married?

I have no choice. My baby can't wait!

It is a good year for marriage for the Monkey. Those who are unattached will find their prospective life partners.

DOG IN THE RAT YEAR

It is not a good year for the Dog. Where career and money are concerned, there will not be any breakthrough. Those born in 1946 will be the most affected.

Except for the winter season, the rest of the year is plagued with problems. The self-employed and salaried workers will have little chance to display their abilities to the fullest.

There is a danger of separation for those who are romantically involved or married. Tolerance is the keyword.

The Dog may experience discomfort in the excretory system, especially in spring and summer. Windfalls are not forthcoming for the Dog this year.

OX

The Ox is considered the 'self-sacrificing deity' by some nationalities. It carts, ploughs, and is by itself a source of food. All this makes the Ox one of the most important animals in the farming community which regarded it as a precious asset.

THE OX YEAR

Lunar Calendar	Element	Solar Calendar
1901	Earth	19 Feb 1901 - 07 Feb 1902
1913	Wood	06 Feb 1913 - 25 Jan 1914
1925	Metal	24 Jan 1925 - 12 Feb 1926
1937	Water	11 Feb 1937 - 30 Jan 1938
1949	Fire	29 Jan 1949 - 16 Feb 1950
1961	Earth	15 Feb 1961 - 04 Feb 1962
1973	Wood	03 Feb 1973 - 22 Jan 1974
1985	Metal	20 Feb 1985 - 08 Feb 1986
1997	Water	07 Feb 1997 - 27 Jan 1998

CAREER

Reputation means more to the Ox than wealth.

Good fortune arrives late in life for the Ox where career is concerned. He or she is suited to be a doctor, lawyer or writer.

HOSPITAL

COURT

Those born in the Ox year will accomplish much either in their youth or when they are old.

You're real lucky. You're already your own boss at 15 while I managed to be one only when I turned 50.

Hee...

OX IN THE OX YEAR

Where career and wealth are concerned, the Ox will meet with a lot of obstacles in the Ox year. Any kind of plans should be carried out in the first half of the year.

I see trouble ahead for you.

You can say that again. I forgot my wallet.

February, March and May are auspicious months for the Ox, especially those born in 1949 and 1961. The worst periods are July, September and December. Avoid financial speculation and gambling.

Where are you going, Miss ?

There is a constant threat of a third party ruining a relationship or marriage. To avoid being cheated, refrain from giving too much in a relationship.

REGISTRY OF MARRIAGES

Didn't you say you were going to marry me?

I'm sorry, but she needs me more.

24

RAT IN THE OX YEAR

It will be a plain sailing year for the Rat with good prospects in career and wealth. Extra care has to be taken when dealing with anything in May and November.

GOOD LUCK

This is a good year to push on with the career for the self-employed and salaried worker. Avoid being arrogant and keep a low profile.

Do you know that my old man is worth more than $10 million?

Did you hear that?

We're kidnapers.

The Rat will find this a good year for romance and marriage, but the married male should refrain from straying lest he loses both his career and money.

How dare you seduce my wife! You're fired!

I'm finished!

Health-wise, the Rat should be wary of illnesses caused by fatigue. The spring season may bring about skin allergies.

Don't touch me, I'm having skin allergy.

25

RABBIT IN THE OX YEAR

The Ox year will be one of frustration for the Rabbit.

?

TROUBLE

Both the self-employed and salaried workers will find it difficult to push on with their careers. Furthermore, there is the danger of running into debts, getting hit by lawsuits or falling ill.

No!

Whaaa...!

Repay your debt or I'll take your daughter away!

It is a year of unhappiness for married couples and those romantically involved. Frequent quarrels may lead to separation.

Whose strand of hair is this?

Ouch!

Besides experiencing stress and painful joints, the Rabbit is also prone to accidents. Avoid travelling long distance.

My leg joint hurts!

DRAGON IN THE OX YEAR

It will be a year of mixed fortunes for the Dragon.

Salaried workers may find it difficult to get a satisfactory job.

Don't look down on me. I'm a graduate.

Avoid dwelling too much on past relationships.

Though we broke up 3 years ago, I remember you still owe me $200.

Watch out for accidents in September.

SNAKE IN
THE OX YEAR

The Snake will sail through the Ox year without a hitch. There are prospects for venturing overseas for those working and good academic results for those still in school. Money will also be forthcoming.

Plain
Sailing

Expanding the business or getting a promotion is easy if the Snake proceeds in a bold, but cautious manner. This is especially true for those born in 1953 and 1965.

Those born in 1941 and 1977 should refrain from overworking lest they be stricken by illnesses that may require surgery. The very young and very old in the family may fall sick easily or have minor accidents.

PROMOTION

cough!

cough!

It will be a year of hits and misses for the Snake where romance is concerned. Those you have no feelings for will go after you while the one you love likes to equate marriage with money.

ROOSTER IN THE OX YEAR

It is a smooth sailing year for the Rooster whose wishes will generally come true. Good luck coupled with hard work will bring about substantial gains.

No one is around ....!

Plain Sailing

The female will meet her benefactor who is of the opposite sex. Career and money prospects are good. For the male, spring and summer are the best times to get romantically involved.

With me around, you won't have any problems.

Benefactor

Most of the months this year are unfavourable to the Rooster. Be extra careful in February and December for there will be quarrels or even financial losses.

x, y, z!
¤,¥,Ø!

Apart from minor problems in the excretory system, the Rooster will enjoy a clean bill of health:

Ngg...!

33

DOG IN THE OX YEAR

This is an inauspicious year for the Dog who may suffer financial losses and get into other kinds of trouble. Those born in 1946 and 1958 should be extra careful.

What comes easily will go as easily. Avoid gambling and financial speculation, particularly in summer and autumn.

Those who are married should spend more time with their spouses to prevent a third party from coming into the picture.

Don't tell me you're going in there too?

Allergies and injuries caused by accidents are some of the health hazards to look out for. Avoid dangerous sports.

TIGER

Man called it the 'King of Beasts' and accorded great respect to it. Legend has it that the Tiger was the incarnation of a celestial general. It is believed to be highly intelligent and possess supernatural powers.

THE TIGER YEAR

Lunar Calendar	Element	Solar Calendar
1902	Metal	08 Feb 1902 - 28 Jan 1903
1914	Water	26 Jan 1914 - 13 Feb 1915
1926	Fire	13 Feb 1926 - 01 Feb 1927
1938	Earth	31 Jan 1938 - 18 Feb 1939
1950	Wood	17 Feb 1950 - 05 Feb 1951
1962	Metal	05 Feb 1962 - 24 Jan 1963
1974	Water	23 Jan 1974 - 10 Feb 1975
1986	Fire	09 Feb 1986 - 28 Jan 1987
1998	Earth	28 Jan 1998 - 15 Feb 1999

41

TIGER IN THE
TIGER YEAR

Overall, this is a stable year for the Tiger, but try not to set your expectations too high or you'll be spreading yourself too thin.

Since you're ill, you should see a doctor.

Where do I find time? I have to work, take care of my kids and do household chores.

Be wary of trouble from colleagues or subordinates. Those born in 1950 and 1962 in particular may find themselves being betrayed by people working for them.

All right, who did this?

Be extra careful in July as a wrong decision may result in financial losses.

You spent $1000 on a piece of rock? You've been cheated, you fool!

Tung!

RAT IN THE TIGER YEAR

The Rat should avoid making investments on the whim in the Tiger year. Watch out for cash-flow problems and budget wisely.

The best thing to do with money is to save it!

Salaried workers will have more luck than the self-employed. Employers will be bogged down by endless problems like manpower shortage.

Only one applicant.

Position wanted delivery man

Those who were born in 1948 will have a windfall or unexpected good news coming their way in December.

Stay rational and refrain from being overly-serious in a relationship. Separate romance from work to prevent others from taking advantage of you.

You've won the top prize in lottery! Let's get married!

Didn't you just say you wanted to break up with me?

I'll help you date Miss Tan if you sign the contract.

RABBIT IN THE TIGER YEAR

It is a plain sailing year for the Rabbit. Career and money prospects are particularly rewarding.

I'll pick this one!

Plain Sailing

However, the Rabbit can easily become inattentive and moody, so plenty of rest is recommended. In August, watch out for dangers and financial losses.

I'm booking you for speeding!

Romance is in the air for the Rabbit. The males will worry about their choice of spouse.

This one has an angelic face while the other possesses a knockout figure. Which one should I choose?

Problems in the digestive system, constipation and backache are the Rabbit's common complaints this year.

Your intestine has become useless. Can I have it?

No way!

SNAKE IN THE TIGER YEAR

The Snake will have quite a tough time in the Tiger year. You will find it more rewarding to do everything yourself.

Please let me go!.

The self-employed and salaried workers should act within the confines of their own abilities. Do not trust anyone blindly lest you get cheated. Spring is a bad season for the Snake.

This drug enables you to grow your own hands and legs. It's only $1000 per bottle.

The Snake will find a suitable life partner easily, but marriage has to wait as this is not a good year to tie the knot.

This year we talk about love, not marriage.

Watch out for headaches, stomach upsets and heart-related problems. Those born in 1953 may have to undergo surgery.

I shouldn't have eaten that spiky creature! I'm in great pain now!

Hedgehog

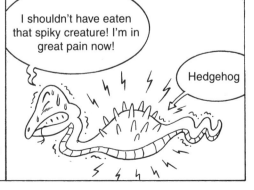

HORSE IN THE TIGER YEAR

This is a particularly rewarding year for the Horse. The best time to proceed with your ambition is in spring and summer.

Good Fortune

However, playing safe is still the best policy. Avoid excessive spending. Luck will wane a little for the Horse in autumn and winter. Those born in 1942 should be wary of getting into trouble with the law over tax-related matters in autumn.

You're hereby found guilty and fined $1000!

PAK!

....

Romance will be smooth sailing, but avoid ruining a perfect relationship in a moment of fickleness.

Will you marry me? Wow!

Health-wise, watch out for backaches and problems of the digestive system.

Crack!

48

MONKEY IN THE TIGER YEAR

This is just not the Monkey's year. You will find yourself being ostracised by your colleagues and friends. Trouble, in the form of squabbles or rumours, will plague you.

I don't like you !

..... ? !

There is a strong sign of substantial loss of money, so stay away from financial speculation.

Your shares have dropped by a dollar!

There goes my everything!

Where affairs of the heart are concerned, your lover or spouse may choose to leave you. Males born in 1957 should watch out for signs of their wives' infidelity.

You're penniless now, so why would I stick around with you?

Common health complaints for the Monkey are eye diseases and limb-related illnesses which tend to prolong.

mirror

My eyes are turning jaundiced. Maybe I've been reading too many naughty magazines.

DOG IN THE TIGER YEAR

Things will go smoothly for the Dog in the Tiger year. Career and money prospects are to your satisfaction.

With me around, everything will be plain sailing for you!

The self-employed will enjoy abundant gains while salaried workers will gain recognition in their workplace. Better luck is in store for the Dog in the summer months.

Keep up the good work!

He's working so hard. It will be a matter of time before he takes over my post as manager.

Romantic encounters may lead to marriages for those born in the Dog year.

Minor illnesses of the digestive system in autumn and winter aside, the Dog will be generally healthy.

How I long to eat dog intestines!

It's just a minor problem. Surely, there's no need for surgery?

RABBIT

A gentle animal, the Rabbit embodies the qualities of purity and beauty. It symbolises the coming of spring - the season where living things take on a new lease of life.

THE RABBIT YEAR

Lunar Calendar	Element	Solar Calendar
1903	Metal	29 Jan 1903 - 15 Feb 1904
1915	Water	14 Feb 1915 - 02 Feb 1916
1927	Fire	02 Feb 1927 - 22 Jan 1928
1939	Earth	19 Feb 1939 - 07 Feb 1940
1951	Wood	06 Feb 1951 - 26 Jan 1952
1963	Metal	25 Jan 1963 - 12 Feb 1964
1975	Water	11 Feb 1975 - 30 Jan 1976
1987	Fire	29 Jan 1987 - 16 Feb 1988
1999	Earth	16 Feb 1999 - 04 Feb 2000

OX IN THE RABBIT YEAR

The Ox will face a number of obstacles and setbacks this year. However, things will improve after autumn, so be patient in spring and summer.

It's so heavy!

Keep your emotions aside when dealing with people and avoid lending money to or acting as a guarantor for others. Otherwise, you will get into trouble with the law. This is especially true for those born in 1949.

We must arrest you since you are the guarantor for the man who broke the law and ran away.

Lovers and spouses tend to be temperamental, so frequent squabbles may take place.

I want Chinese food!

I prefer Western!

The common health complaints for the Ox are headaches and insomnia.

Another sleepless night!

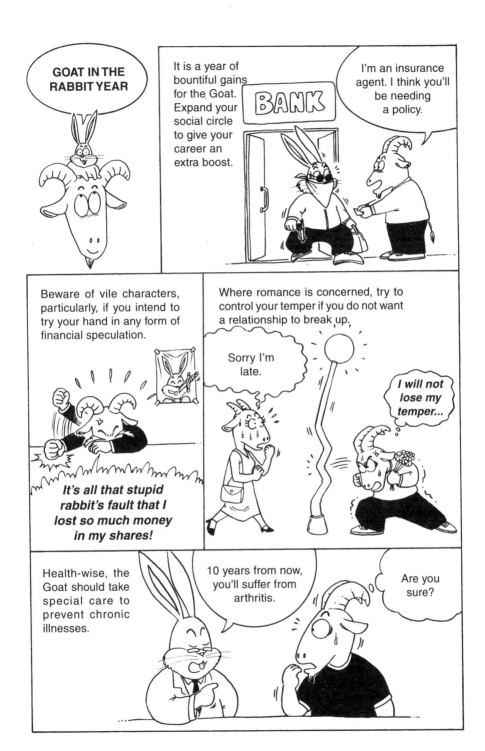

MONKEY IN THE RABBIT YEAR

The Monkey will be caught in a number of squabbles this year. Be on your guard.

He's going to get it from us the moment he comes out.

Be careful in everything you do. Otherwise, you will get cheated.

I've got your money, but I'm not going to marry you. Bye, bye!

Honey, don't go!

The path to romance is full of hiccups for the Monkey. You will only be asking for trouble if you persist in being stubborn.

I asked her out first!

Do you want to fight it out?

Health-wise, observe food hygiene and watch out for inflammation of the digestive system in February and June.

HELP!

PIG IN THE RABBIT YEAR

The Pig will find this a year of difficulties. Beware of being cheated or sold out by others.

I should not have trusted you! You sold me a fake!

Career and money propects alternate between good and bad during spring and summer. Think carefully before you invest in anything.

You should have bought this plot of land when I told you too. Look what you've lost!

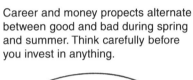

Where romance is concerned, a fruitful relationship will come your way this year.

I never expected us to meet this way.

Health-wise, you are not as strong as before. Common complaints are headaches, insomnia and nausea.

DRAGON

The only mythological animal among the twelve, the Dragon is no less important than the others. Stories about it can be found everywhere. Man has long considered it a celestial creature and looked upon it with awe and respect.

THE DRAGON YEAR

Lunar Calendar	Element	Solar Calendar
1904	Fire	16 Feb 1904 - 03 Feb 1905
1916	Earth	03 Feb 1916 - 22 Jan 1917
1928	Wood	23 Jan 1928 - 09 Feb 1929
1940	Metal	08 Feb 1940 - 26 Jan 1941
1952	Water	27 Jan 1952 - 13 Feb 1953
1964	Fire	13 Feb 1964 - 01 Feb 1965
1976	Earth	31 Jan 1976 - 17 Feb 1977
1988	Wood	17 Feb 1988 - 05 Feb 1989
2000	Metal	05 Feb 2000 - 23 Jan 2001

PERSONALITY

People born in the Dragon year possess exceptional qualities like what is told in mythical folklore. They are refined, respectable and have a sacred air about them.

He doesn't look the lest bit respectable.

Give me back my toy!

The Dragon is easy-going, willing to take risks, but tends to be more stubborn than most in his thinking and behaviour.

Don't get yourself killed!

Let me go! I'm trying to save him!

HELP!!

Full of imagination and possessing an indomitable spirit, the Dragon is decisive when it comes to dealing with anything.

Though the Dragon has the potential for accomplishing great things, he is not easily accepted by others.

Warm, curious and helpful by nature, the Dragon is often mistaken for being meddlesome.

75

HORSE IN THE DRAGON YEAR

The Horse must persist in taking the initiative and be decisive to make the Dragon year a gainful year. Otherwise, things will go downhill for you.

Be level-headed and do not leave everything to luck. Greed will only bring you trouble. Push on with whatever plans you have in spring and summer so that when bad luck hits you in autumn and winter, you will be prepared.

There is a danger of married couples getting involved in scandalous affairs.

Health-wise, you may suffer from ailments of the digestive and circulatory systems.

I'll teach you to seduce my husband!

I wonder whose side I should be on.

Aren't you a bit too old to get pregnant?

Stop uttering nonsense! I'm just suffering from indigestion.

ROOSTER IN THE DRAGON YEAR

This is a lucky and prosperous year for the Rooster. Career and money prospects are to your expectations.

Hee! Hee! I managed to fool yet another.

I'm counting on you.

You cannot afford to be careless when dealing with colleagues or friends. Otherwise, you will end up making the wrong decisions. There are signs of financial losses due to carelessness in autumn and winter.

He wrote an extra zero on my cheque for $100! I'm rich!

Huh!!

Where affairs of the heart are concerned, you will meet with a number of setbacks. Relationships are shortlived, so avoid putting in too much. Females may fall for married men.

Let's get married.

But I'm already married.

You will be in the pink of health, but take special care in autumn lest you dislocate a bone or joint.

Tak!

PIG IN THE DRAGON YEAR

This is a stable year for the Pig with good career and money prospects. It is also a good time to venture beyond your usual scope.

Lately, you've been coming home very late.

Didn't you tell me to venture outside?

For salaried workers, it is advisable to stay away from gambling and financial speculation.

Things will be relatively peaceful for you except for July where there are signs of financial mishap taking place at your own home.

The good news for this month is I had a raise of $200; the bad news, I gambled away $400.

What the....!

This is a good year for courting couples to get married. Those who are single will meet their ideal life partners. Females born in 1959 should avoid getting involved in a love triangle. You get toothache and experience discomfort in your digestive system.

SNAKE

Though the very mention of the word 'snake' sends shivers down many a spine, it is unfair to generalise and say that all snakes are evil. In the Chinese mythical classic entitled Legend Of The White Snake, the two characters, White Snake and Green Snake symbolise kindness and virtue. However, the Bible refers to it as the cunning and treacherous demon or devil.

THE SNAKE YEAR

Lunar Calendar	Element	Solar Calendar
1905	Fire	04 Feb 1905 - 24 Jan 1906
1917	Earth	23 Jan 1917 - 10 Feb 1918
1929	Wood	10 Feb 1929 - 29 Jan 1930
1941	Metal	27 Jan 1941 - 14 Feb 1942
1953	Water	14 Feb 1953 - 02 Feb 1954
1965	Fire	02 Feb 1965 - 20 Jan 1966
1977	Earth	18 Feb 1977 - 06 Feb 1978
1989	Wood	06 Feb 1989 - 26 Jan 1990

95

TIGER IN THE SNAKE YEAR

The Tiger's luck wanes in the Snake year. Where career is concerned, your gains will not be proportional to the great efforts you put in.

That's odd. My business has expanded, yet my takings remain the same.

Money comes and goes easily. Avoid gambling and financial speculation.

Dad, could you lend me some money?

What do you do with your pay every month?

Though you have a likeable personality, it will still be quite some time before you find true love.

I have everything except a wife.

You are in the pink of health at the beginning of the year, but after the May, there are signs of deterioration. Observe food hygiene and take precaution against illnesses of the liver.

RABBIT IN THE SNAKE YEAR

Underlying dangers await the Rabbit in the Snake year. Do not trust others too easily.

Your son has been arrested. He wants me to get money from you to pay for his bail.

In April and May be wary of vile characters around you.

He was the one who told me not to trust you.

Where romance is concerned, there are definite possibilities. However, your stubbornness makes it difficult for you to find someone you love.

You will be relatively healthy, but watch out for the flu and migraine.

Let me be your Miss Right.

I hate creepy crawlies.

She'll eat me up anytime.

Ha... Choo..!

HORSE IN THE
SNAKE YEAR

This is a particularly rewarding year for the Horse. Though you will meet with a lot of pressure and competition in your work, luck is on your side.

Romance will be one big roller-coaster ride for you. One moment, you and your partner are at your most loving, the next, you behave like mortal enemies.

You are generally in good health this year though you may occasionally suffer from indigestion, insomnia or stress.

107

HORSE

The Horse is one of man's best friends. It has a beautifully-shaped body, strong, sturdy legs and a glorious mane. Its strong and independent character can be seen from the way it struggles to stand up and walk barely ten minutes after it is born.

THE HORSE YEAR

Lunar Calendar	Element	Solar Calendar
1906	Water	25 Jan 1906 - 12 Feb 1907
1918	Fire	11 Feb 1918 - 31 Jan 1919
1930	Earth	30 Jan 1930 - 16 Feb 1931
1942	Wood	15 Feb 1942 - 04 Feb 1943
1954	Metal	03 Feb 1954 - 23 Jan 1955
1966	Water	21 Jan 1966 - 04 Feb 1967
1978	Fire	07 Feb 1978 - 27 Jan 1979
1990	Earth	27 Jan 1990 - 14 Feb 1991

110

111

ROMANCE

Those born in the Horse year are straightforward in their attitude when it comes to romance. It is normal for them to marry young and divorce young.

I got married at 15, divorced at 16 and remarried at 17.

You were so spunky, Grandma!

Because of their love for freedom and strongheaded personality, they clash with others frequently. Though they can be good friends and lovers, it will not be a long-lasting thing.

La! La! La!

Shut up! You sound horrible!

No, I love it. Carry on.

HORSE IN THE HORSE YEAR

It is a mixed year for the Horse alternating between good and bad. Money comes easily and goes as easily.

Ha! I found $100!

Career will be plain sailing at the beginning of the year. There are signs of financial mishap and conflicts with others in the May and June. Come autumn and winter, the Horse's luck will deteriorate even more. The only way to overcome the crisis you may face is to be tolerant and on your guard.

Come out now or I'll set your house on fire!

Just as well. I'm turning blue from the cold.

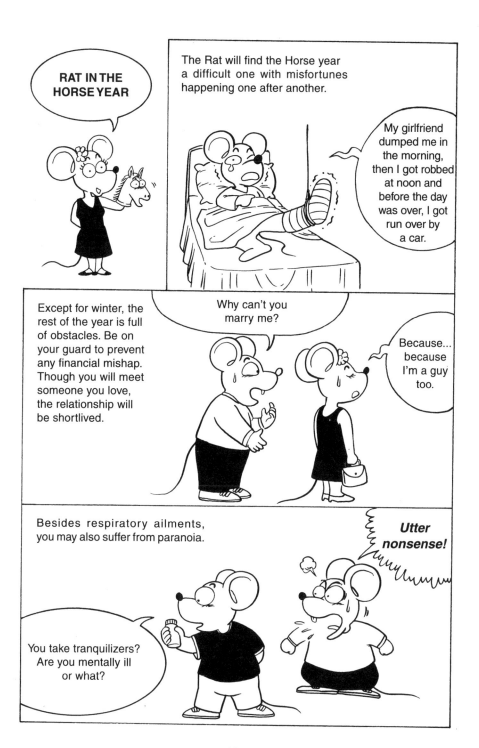

ROOSTER IN THE HORSE YEAR

This is basically a stable year for the Rooster. Salaried workers may find themselves being ostracized by their colleagues while the self-employed may encounter difficulties in business. However, you can weather any crisis by dealing with it in a sure and steady way.

She's selling her duck eggs so cheaply and it's affecting the sale of my eggs. I must do something about this.

Romance-wise, your partner will blow hot and cold, making you very confused. A third party may also break up your relationship.

She was cold to me on Monday, Wednesday and Friday. Then on Tuesday, Thursday and Saturday, she became so passionate. I wonder how she'll treat me on Sunday.

Take preventive measures against colds during winter. Observe good eating habits and watch out for sprains and fractures.

I had to fall ill at a time when I was supposed to play Santa Claus!

I'm going to distribute Christmas presents!

PIG IN THE HORSE YEAR

Though this is a relatively good year for the Pig, care must be taken to prevent acts of sabotage by others arising from jealousy.

I'm first!

Money prospects are good during spring. Come summer, there is a need to budget wisely. In autumn, expand your social circle and take the initiative to improve interpersonal relationships. This will facilitate your career development in winter.

Though your romantic encounters are plenty, there is no sign of a permanent commitment.

Your health will be a problem. You may require medical treatment for your lungs and chest at the beginning and end of the year. Take measures to prevent colds.

This has been a most enjoyable day. Let's do it again some other time.

I'm afraid not. I'm getting married next week.

It's very important that you examine me very carefully, do you understand?

Now, who's the doctor here, you or me?

125

GOAT

People in China regard the Goat as an auspicious animal. Its Chinese character is derived from the character in the word which means 'auspicious'. Legend has it that, when considering animals to be represented in the Chinese horoscope, the Jade Emperor had in mind only the Ox, Dragon and Deer. The Goat was included after it impressed him with its magnificent horns, healthy body and ability to run and jump in the most graceful manner.

THE GOAT YEAR

Lunar Calendar	Element	Solar Calendar
1907	Water	13 Feb 1907 - 01 Feb 1908
1919	Fire	01 Feb 1919 - 19 Feb 1920
1931	Earth	17 Feb 1931 - 05 Feb 1932
1943	Wood	05 Feb 1943 - 24 Jan 1944
1955	Metal	24 Jan 1955 - 11 Feb 1956
1967	Water	09 Feb 1967 - 29 Jan 1968
1979	Fire	28 Jan 1979 - 15 Feb 1980
1991	Earth	15 Feb 1991 - 03 Feb 1992

131

135

DRAGON IN THE GOAT YEAR

The Dragon's fortune alternates between good and bad this year. People around you may give you endless troubles with their gossips.

The best way to shut myself off from the world outside is to wear headphones.

There are signs of setbacks in career and money matters during spring and summer. However, things will look up after autumn.

Give me back my money!

Autumn, where are you?

Though you will find a suitable life partner, your relationship with him or her is fraught with difficulties. You must put in extra effort if you want good results.

I'll marry you provided you have the '5 Cs'.

I already have three 'Cs' and I'll work harder for the other two.

The Dragon is quite accident-prone this year. In winter, your digestive system may give you problems.

Oh no! There's not a toilet in sight!

139

142

143

MONKEY

It is scientifically-proven that man evolved from the ape. Hence, the Monkey, which is part of the ape family, is closely linked to man. It is the most intelligent, agile and capable animal of its kind. In addition, its physiological make-up is uncannily similar to man's.

THE MONKEY YEAR

Lunar Calendar	Element	Solar Calendar
1908	Earth	02 Feb 1908 - 21 Jan 1909
1920	Wood	20 Feb 1920 - 07 Feb 1921
1932	Metal	06 Feb 1932 - 25 Jan 1933
1944	Water	25 Jan 1944 - 12 Feb 1945
1956	Fire	12 Feb 1956 - 30 Jan 1957
1968	Earth	30 Jan 1968 - 16 Feb 1969
1980	Wood	16 Feb 1980 - 04 Feb 1981
1992	Metal	04 Feb 1992 - 22 Jan 1993

RAT IN THE MONKEY YEAR

The Rat's lucky star shines especially bright this year. Early in the year, money prospects are at its best.

God has been so kind to me!

Salaried workers can look forward to a promotion or raise. However, this is not a good time to change jobs.

You protect me and I'll give you a raise!

You're asking him to protect you? You'll have better luck begging me for mercy!

Health-wise, take precaution against ailments of the digestive system. In spring and summer, watch out for contagious diseases.

Don't eat me! I have contagious disease!

SNAKE IN THE MONKEY YEAR

Though this is not an extremely auspicious year for the Snake, it is not exactly an unlucky one either. Your good money prospects will enable your savings to grow.

What a pity! I won the top prize, but I only placed a $1 bet on it.

Whether you are self-employed or a salaried worker, your career will be closely linked to someone of the opposite sex. It can become better or worse, depending on the help you are getting.

She is our boss' lover. That's why she got promoted to manager soon after she joined our company.

Injuries to your limbs and head may result from accidents. A frightening experience awaits you if you go travelling in summer.

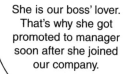

Bungee jumping

Ahhhh!

GOAT IN THE MONKEY YEAR

The Goat will encounter a number of difficulties in the Monkey year. It is not advisable to embark on new business ventures. Be patient and safeguard what you already have.

Oh dear! What should I do with all these extra carrots I bought? They are not selling well at all.

You will meet someone you love, but do not take the relationship for granted or a third party may come along and ruin it.

Your health will be generally good. However, do take precaution against ailments of the digestive system and road accidents.

Pak!

ROOSTER IN THE MONKEY YEAR
This is a year of deceit for the Rooster. Most of the time, things and people are not quite what they appear to be.
Hi, brother!
!!
A wise career move is to venture abroad. The local market is not as lucrative.
Your eggs are not selling well in the local market so I'm looking into foreign sources.
Where romance is concerned, you may find yourself prolonging a relationship unnecessarily. Beware of the intrusion of a third party.
Kiss me!
Er... I haven't brushed my teeth yet.

160

ROOSTER

The Rooster, as told in legends, originated from the many stars that fell onto earth. People sing praises about it as it is believed to possess the five virtues - proficiency in the arts (as represented by its crown), dexterity in sporting activities (the claws of its feet), courage (it would not hesitate to fight its enemy), benevolence (sharing food with others) and trustworthiness (crowing at daybreak without fail).

THE ROOSTER YEAR

Lunar Calendar	Element	Solar Calendar
1909	Earth	22 Jan 1909 - 09 Feb 1910
1921	Wood	08 Feb 1921 - 27 Jan 1922
1933	Metal	26 Jan 1933 - 13 Feb 1934
1945	Water	13 Feb 1945 - 01 Feb 1946
1957	Fire	31 Jan 1957 - 17 Feb 1958
1969	Earth	17 Feb 1969 - 05 Feb 1970
1981	Wood	05 Feb 1981 - 24 Jan 1982
1993	Metal	23 Jan 1993 - 09 Feb 1994

They love to dress up and have a preference for flamboyant clothes.

What a knockout!

Praises and compliments from others are very important to them, but given their strong sense of pride, they do not take too well to criticisms.

Chicken meat is the most delicious.

Compliments like this spook me!

They show enthusiasm in the things they do and will not tolerate sloppiness. As a result, they give others the impression that they are eccentric and nag too much.

Koo ! Koo! Koo!

How dare you wake me up on Sunday morning ?!

The Snake will breeze through the Rooster year. You should go through every document or contract very carefully before signing it.

SNAKE IN THE ROOSTER YEAR

Sign the contract now and we'll go dancing.

My ploy works!

Okay!

Though you will have an interesting love life, a prospective life partner is not forthcoming this year. Married couples should go on a second honeymoon to prevent a marriage crisis.

They were fighting like cats and dogs before they went on a holiday abroad. Now they behave like newly-weds.

Where health is concerned, take precaution against liver ailments. Avoid strenuous exercises to guard against injuries to the limbs.

I'm a snake, so I have no limb injuries to worry about. Hee! Hee!

GOAT IN THE ROOSTER YEAR

Obstacles are in the way of the Goat this year, especially in summer and winter where career and money prospects will hit a snag.

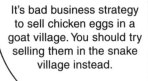

It's bad business strategy to sell chicken eggs in a goat village. You should try selling them in the snake village instead.

Investments should be made only after careful consideration. Take extra care of an elderly member of your family. You may find it difficult to get over your bereavement.

Whaaaa....! Why did you die without leaving me any money ?

Quarrels are rampant in your love life and you will have problems finding true love this year.

I can't stand your smelly feet!

Neither can I stand your body odour!

179

DOG

The close relationship between man and Dog can be traced to primitive times. It is more of a love-hate relationship than anything else. Men love the Dog because it is agile, loyal, intelligent and uncomplaining by nature. However, they hate it for its too eager-to-please ways which borders on hypocrisy.

THE DOG YEAR

Lunar Calendar	Element	Solar Calendar
1910	Metal	10 Feb 1910 - 29 Jan 1911
1922	Water	28 Jan 1922 - 15 Feb 1923
1934	Fire	14 Feb 1934 - 03 Feb 1935
1946	Earth	02 Feb 1946 - 21 Jan 1947
1958	Wood	18 Feb 1958 - 07 Feb 1959
1970	Metal	06 Feb 1970 - 26 Jan 1971
1982	Water	25 Jan 1982 - 12 Feb 1983
1994	Fire	10 Feb 1994 - 30 Jan 1995

People born in the Dog year respect those who respect others. They will not hesitate to stand up for their friends.

Besides being agile, quick-thinking and observant, they also have a great sense of humour and the gift of the gab.

182

189

DRAGON IN THE DOG YEAR

The Dragon will find the Dog year physically and mentally taxing. Particularly frustrating is the disappointing end results despite the efforts you put in.

I forgot the fire-starter!

Darn it! It took me such a long time to get a fire going and now, it's raining!

For salaried workers, this is not a good time to change jobs. Tolerance is the keyword.

Since I haven't found another job, I must put up with him!

Your chances of meeting someone special are quite slim. Married couples should be wary of the intrusion of a third party.

She's so dark! Isn't there a fair-complexioned one amongst them?

SNAKE IN THE DOG YEAR

This is a stable year for the Snake. You may want to push ahead with personal plans. Career and money prospects are at their best in spring and summer.

Where romance is concerned, you may face obstacles in the initial stages of a relationship. After autumn, however, good progress will be made. November is a good time to get married.

She used to treat me with indifference, but after I struck lottery, she has been pestering me to marry her.

Common health complaints for the Snake this year are insomnia, exhaustion and ailments of the digestive system.

I can tell.

Please help me, Doc! I've been counting sheep for the past 15 nights!

HORSE IN THE DOG YEAR

Generally, this is a good year for the Horse. As the saying goes : Harmony breeds prosperity, so how things will turn out for you depends on yourself.

Let me punch you 10 times and this $100 note is yours.

Deal!

Try to maintain a cordial relationship with your colleagues. A promotion or raise may come your way after autumn.

Break it up! The boss is here!

Health-wise, watch out for problems in the blood circulation system and heart ailments.

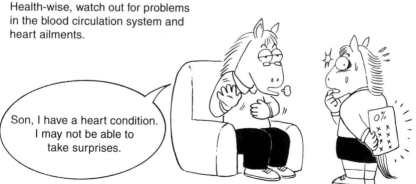

Son, I have a heart condition. I may not be able to take surprises.

MONKEY IN
THE DOG YEAR

This is the year to be conservative and on your guard for the Monkey. Be warned of the many obstacles you will encounter, especially in spring. Deal with them very carefully.

As far as possible, try not to get involved in matters that do not concern you at all to prevent trouble and losses.

Avoid visiting the sick or attending funerals. Health-wise, take precaution against ailments of the digestive and respiratory systems. In spring, watch out for road accidents.

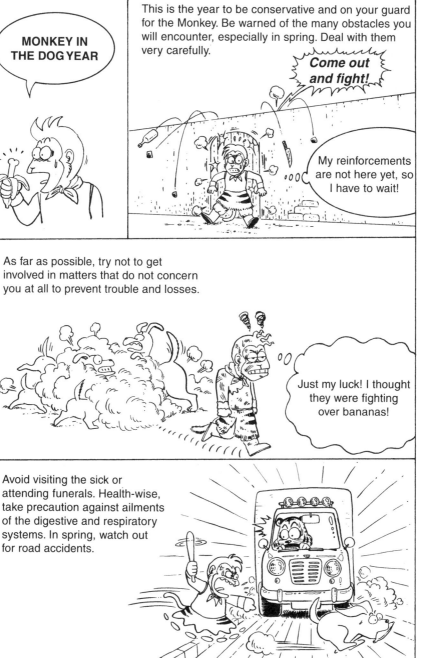

PIG

'Where there are people, there are pigs'- it goes to show how closely linked the two are. The Pig is said to have originated from the North Star which fell onto earth to bring good fortune to mankind. Nasty things have been said about the Pig; that it is stupid, lazy and greedy. However, science has proven that this is not the case. In fact, what the Dog can do, the Pig can do better if not as well.

THE PIG YEAR

Lunar Calendar	Element	Solar Calendar
1911	Metal	30 Jan 1911 - 17 Feb 1912
1923	Water	16 Feb 1923 - 04 Feb 1924
1935	Fire	04 Feb 1935 - 23 Jan 1936
1947	Earth	22 Jan 1947 - 09 Feb 1948
1959	Wood	08 Feb 1959 - 27 Jan 1960
1971	Metal	27 Jan 1971 - 14 Feb 1972
1983	Water	13 Feb 1983 - 01 Feb 1984
1995	Fire	31 Jan 1995 - 18 Feb 1996

205

215

EPILOGUE: THE LINK BETWEEN THE ANIMALS AND ONE'S FATE

You need to combine the hour, day, month and year of your birth, fortunate stem, harmonious branch, yin and yang, and element in order to arrive at an accurate prediction.

Hour of birth
Fortunate stem
Harmonious Branch
Yin or Yang
$+$ **Element**

$=$

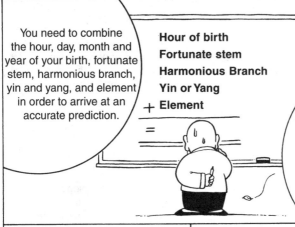

Here in this book, the characteristics of each animal and the type of fortune they represent should only be used as the basic principle from where you proceed to master the more detailed and profound aspects of Chinese astrology.

Like all things in the cosmic world, the life of an individual follows a certain order. Life and death, growth and decay - these are the unchanging laws of nature. The same goes with the link between fate and the 12 animals in Chinese astrology.

We do!

So, do you still believe in the link between one's fate and the 12 animal-signs?

I don't!

Other Asiapac Titles:
Chinese Art of Divination

THE I CHING

The I Ching is one of the oldest classics in the world and is widely regarded as a storehouse of wisdom for guidance in the conduct of life. This comic edition is designed for practical use and seeks to unravel the mystery of The I Ching by exploring the origins and explaining the applications of the ancient art of divination.

FENG SHUI KIT:
The Chinese Way to Health, Wealth and Happiness, at Home and at Work

The *book* contains full instructions and draws upon the wisdom of Man-Ho Kwok, one of the few fully qualified feng shui masters living in Europe. Use the *feng shui compass* to discover quickly and easily the best position for everything. And discover how to place the *pa kua mirror* provided to deflect any malign forces and spirits.

Asiapac Comic Series (by Tsai Chih Chung)

Art of War
Translated by Leong Weng Kam
The Art of War provides a compact set of principles essential for victory in battles; applicable to military strategists, in business and human relationships.

Book of Zen
Translated by Koh Kok Kiang
Zen makes the art of spontaneous living the prime concern of the human being. Tsai depicts Zen with unfettered versatility; his illustrations spans a period of more than 2,000 years.

Da Xue
Translated by Mary Ng En Tzu
The second book in the Four Books of the Confucian Classics. It sets forth the higher principles of moral science and advocates that the cultivation of the person be the first thing attended to in the process of the pacification of kingdoms.

Fantasies of the Six Dynasties
Translated by Jenny Lim
Tsai Chih Chung has creatively illustrated and annotated 19 bizarre tales of human encounters with supernatural beings which were compiled during the Six Dyansties (AD 220-589).

Lun Yu
Translated by Mary Ng En Tzu
A collection of the discourses of Confucius, his disciples and others on various topics. Several bits of choice sayings have been illustrated for readers in this book.

New Account of World Tales
Translated by Alan Chong
These 120 selected anecdotes tell the stories of emperors, princes, high officials, generals, courtiers, urbane monks and lettered gentry of a turbulent time. They afford a stark and amoral insight into human behaviour in its full spectrum of virtues and frailties and glimpses of brilliant Chinese witticisms, too.

Origins of Zen
Translated by Koh Kok Kiang
Tsai in this book traces the origins and development of Zen in China with a light-hearted touch which is very much in keeping with the Zen spirit of absolute freedom and unbounded creativity.

Records of the Historian
Translated by Tang Nguok Kiong
Adapted from Records of the Historian, one of the greatest historical work China has produced, Tsai has illustrated the life and characteristics of the Four Lords of the Warring Strates.

Roots of Wisdom
Translated by Koh Kok Kiang
One of the gems of Chinese literature, whose advocacy of a steadfast nature and a life of simplicity, goodness, quiet joy and harmony with one's fellow beings and the world at large has great relevance in an age of rapid changes.

Sayings of Confucius
Translated by Goh Beng Choo
This book features the life of Confucius, selected sayings from The Analects and some of his more prominent pupils. It captures the warm relationship between the sage and his disciples, and offers food for thought for the modern readers.

Sayings of Han Fei Zi
Translated by Alan Chong
Tsai Chih Chung retold and interpreted the basic ideas of legalism, a classical political philosophy that advocates a draconian legal code, embodying a system of liberal reward and heavy penalty as the basis of government, in his unique style.

Sayings of Lao Zi
Translated by Koh Kok Kiang & Wong Lit Khiong
The thoughts of Lao Zi, the founder of Taoism, are presented here in a light-hearted manner. It features the selected sayings from Dao De Jing.

Sayings of Lao Zi Book 2
Translated by Koh Kok Kiang
In the second book, Tsai Chih Chung has tackled some of the more abstruse passages from the Dao De Jing which he has not included in the first volume of Sayings of Lao Zi.

Sayings of Lie Zi
Translated by Koh Kok Kiang
A famous Taoist sage whose sayings deals with universal themes such as the joy of living, reconciliation with death, the limitations of human knowledge, the role of chance events.

Sayings of Mencius
Translated by Mary Ng En Tzu
This book contains stories about the life of Mencius and various excerpts from "Mencius", one of the Four Books of the Confucian Classics, which contains the philosophy of Mencius.

Sayings of Zhuang Zi
Translated by Goh Beng Choo
Zhuang Zi's non-conformist and often humorous views of life have been creatively illustrated and simply presented by Tsai Chih Chung in this book.

Sayings of Zhuang Zi Book 2
Translated by Koh Kok Kiang
Zhuang Zi's book is valued for both its philosophical insights and as a work of great literary merit. Tsai's second book on Zhuang Zi shows maturity in his unique style.

Strange Tales of Liaozhai
Translated by Tang Nguok Kiong
In this book, Tsai Chih Chung has creatively illustrated 12 stories from the Strange Tales of Liaozhai, an outstanding Chinese classic written by Pu Songling in the early Qing Dynasty.

Zhong Yong
Translated by Mary Ng En Tzu
Zhong Yong, written by Zi Si, the grandson of Confucius, gives voice to the heart of the discipline of Confucius. Tsai has presented it in a most readable manner for the modern readers to explore with great delight.

100 Series Art Album

100 Celebrated Chinese Women

Artist Lu Yanguang captures the spirit of some of China's most influential and famous women. Spanning over two thousand years of China's history, the characters in this collection reflect the many and varied roles which women have played throughout the ages.

100 Chinese Gods

Lu Yanguang has interpreted Chinese gods, goddesses and immortals with imagination and intelligence.

A comprehensive range is represented: from the superior Jade Emperor to the fearsome King Yama of Hell; from the compassionate Midwife Goddess to the ordinary men who through practising Taoism attained immortality and joined the ranks of Heaven.

Strategy & Leadership Series by Wang Xuanming

Thirty-six Stratagems: Secret Art of War
Translated by Koh Kok Kiang (cartoons) &
Liu Yi (text of the stratagems)
 A Chinese military classic which emphasizes deceptive schemes to achieve military objectives. It has attracted the attention of military authorities and general readers alike.

Six Strategies for War: The Practice of Effective Leadership
Translated by Alan Chong
 A powerful book for rulers, administrators and leaders, it covers critical areas in management and warfare including: how to recruit talents and manage the state; how to beat the enemy and build an empire; how to lead wisely; and how to manoeuvre brilliantly.

Gems of Chinese Wisdom: Mastering the Art of Leadership
Translated by Leong Weng Kam
 Wise up with this delightful collection of tales and anecdotes on the wisdom of great men and women in Chinese history, including Confucius, Meng Changjun and Gou Jian.

Three Strategies of Huang Shi Gong: The Art of Government
Translated by Alan Chong
 Reputedly one of man's oldest monograph on military strategy, it unmasks the secrets behind brilliant military manoeuvres, clever deployment and control of subordinates, and effective government.

100 Strategies of War: Brilliant Tactics in Action
Translated by Yeo Ai Hoon
 The book captures the essence of extensive military knowledge and practice, and explores the use of psychology in warfare, the importance of building diplomatic relations with the enemy's neighbours, the use of espionage and reconnaissance, etc.

Latest Titles in
Strategy & Leadership Series

Chinese Business Strategies

The Chinese are known for being shrewd businessmen able to thrive under the toughest market conditions. The secret of their success lies in 10 time-tested principles of Chinese entrepreneurship.

This book offers readers 30 real-life, ancient case studies with comments on their application in the context of modern business.

Sixteen Strategies of Zhuge Liang

Zhuge Liang, the legendary statesman and military commander during the Three Kingdoms Period, is the epitome of wisdom.

Well-grounded in military principles of Sun Zi and other masters before him, he excelled in applying them in state administration and his own innovations, thus winning many spectacular victories with his uncanny anticipation of enemy moves.

SPECIAL OFFER

Strategy & Leadership Series

- [ ] Chinese Business Strategies
- [ ] Three Strategies of Huang Shi Gong
- [ ] Six Strategies for War
- [ ] Sixteen Strategies of Zhuge Liang
- [ ] Thirty-six Stratagems
- [ ] 100 Strategies of War
- [ ] Gems of Chinese Wisdom

Make your subscription for any 5 volumes or more of this comic series (tick box) and enjoy **20% discount**.

Original Price: S$15.90 per volume (*exclusive* of GST)

Offer at special discount (*inclusive of* postage):-

	5 Volumes	6 Volumes	7 Volumes
Singapore	68.30	82.20	95.30
Malaysia	71.60	88.30	101.00
International-by sea mail	78.60	100.30	113.00

* All Prices in Singapore Dollars. 3% GST charge for local orders.

I wish to subscribe for the above-mentioned titles

at the nett price of **S$**_____ (*inclusive of* postage)

- [ ] **For Singapore orders only:**
  Enclosed is my postal order/money order/cheque/ for **S$** _____

  (No.: _____)

For Singapore/Malaysia/International orders:

- [ ] Credit card. Please charge the amount of SIN$_____ to my credit card

VISA [ ] Card No. _____ Card Holder's Name _____

MASTER [ ] Expiry Date_____ Order Date_____ Signature _____

Name _____

Address _____

_____ **Tel** _____

Send to: ASIAPAC BOOKS PTE LTD 629 Aljunied Road #04-06 Cititech Industrial Building
          Singapore 389838 Tel: 65 -7453868 Fax: 65 -7453822

Note:

For this offer of 20% discount, there is no restriction on the titles ordered, that is, you may order any 5 or more of the series. Prices are subject to change without prior notice.

《亞太漫畫系列》

十二生肖

原著：戴添祥
繪畫：廖榮鑫
翻譯：丘惠芳

亞太圖書有限公司出版